Contents

Introduction 4

Rocket, before 1232...6

Telescope, before 1608...8

Liquid-fuelled rocket, 1926 10

Radio telescope, 1937 12

Satellite, 1957 14

Space probe, 1959 16

Weather and resources satellites, 1960.........................18

Spy and navigation satellites, 1960 20

Manned spacecraft, 1961...22

Spacesuit, 1961 24

Moon rocket, 1969 26

Moon lander, 1969..28

Space rover, 1970 30

Space food and fitness, 1971 32

Space station, 1971...34

Mars lander, 1976...36

Space Shuttle, 1981 38

Jet pack, 1984 40

Space telescope, 1990 42

Timeline...44

Glossary 46

Index 48

Introduction

Space begins beyond the limits of the Earth's atmosphere – the blanket of gases that wraps the planet in a warm, life-giving layer. Space is cold and airless, stretching into infinity beyond the height at which jet airliners fly –10 to 12 kilometres – and the highest point reached by balloons – about 40 kilometres. To travel into space requires engines that do not need outside air to burn fuel, but can reach very high speeds to escape the pull of Earth's **gravity**. To survive in the emptiness of space, human explorers need to carry an 'Earth environment' with them, in the form of life-support systems to supply air, water and food, and remove or recycle waste.

First dreams of space

People dreamed about travelling in space long before there were machines capable of taking them there. It was not until the 1500s that scientists understood how the planets moved in paths, or **orbits**, around the Sun. In the early 1600s they got their first closer look at the Moon and the nearest planets through primitive telescopes.

Jules Verne and other science-fiction writers created fantastic voyages through space and time, in which ships might sail to the Moon!

In 1865 the French writer Jules Verne wrote a science-fiction story called *From the Earth to the Moon* in which people went to the Moon in a craft fired from a huge cannon. Space travel became one of the most popular subjects for science-fiction writers. After the first aeroplane took to the skies in 1903, it seemed only a matter of time before real-life explorers matched the adventures of the fictional space-fliers.

The inventions that made space-flight happen

No single inventor made space-flight happen. There are no Wright brothers, no Karl Benz, no Thomas Edison in the history of space invention. Teams of scientists produced thousands of inventions to make the new technology work. Key inventions, such as telescopes and rockets, helped scientists to learn more about the **solar system** and the myriads of **galaxies**, or star-groups, in the universe.

Space-flight was impossible before 1900 because no means of flying into space existed. In the early 20th century, a handful of pioneers and amateurs swapped ideas about how space might be explored. In the 1940s, military demands during the Second World War speeded up work on new inventions such as rockets, nuclear power, computers and **radar**. In 1945 science writer Arthur C Clarke suggested that space satellites might be used for worldwide radio and TV communication.

Teamwork

By the 1950s teams of scientists and engineers, most of them working in the United States and the **Soviet Union**, were building big rockets. In 1957 a rocket launched the first tiny satellite. The 'space race' brought rapid advances in **electronics**, computers, medicine and long-range communications.

The human space-fliers or **astronauts** (called **cosmonauts** by the Russians) made the headlines. The scientists and engineers – who made everything from Moon boots and space pens to giant rockets and robot planet-crawlers – remained in the background. For every Moon-walker on TV, there were hundreds of people on the ground at Mission Control. Space exploration is a team effort and very expensive. This is why the latest space venture, the *International Space Station*, is a multi-national project.

Rocket, before 1232

Rockets were invented in China, probably soon after the invention of **gunpowder** some time before AD 1000, but their inventor is unknown. History books tell how the Chinese used 'arrows of flying fire' to fight off the Mongols in AD 1232 – some of the first war rockets. Chinese inventors had made fireworks by filling paper or wooden tubes with gunpowder. Someone added a stick for balance, lit the bottom end, and when the tube whizzed into the air in a shower of sparks, the rocket was born.

The rocket's development

By the end of the 1200s, rockets were being used in battles across Asia and as far west as Spain. Inventors came up with crazy ideas for using rocket power. They dreamed up rocket-driven rams to batter down castle walls and rocket torpedoes to skim across the sea and wreck enemy ships. A Chinese legend tells how, in about 1500, a man named Wan Hu tried to fly by tying 47 rockets – and himself – to two large kites. He disappeared in the explosion!

Congreve rockets made a lot of noise and smoke, which added to their terrifying effect. Their 'red glare' is mentioned in the words of the US national anthem.

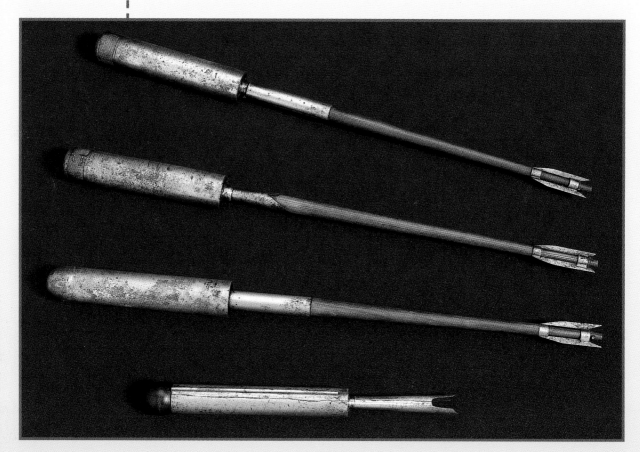

In the 1600s a Polish inventor, Kazimierz Siemienowicz, drew remarkable sketches of different rockets – a **step rocket**, a cluster of rockets strapped together, and a rocket with wings. These drawings pre-dated 20th-century rockets by 300 years. Also in the 1600s the British scientist Isaac Newton explained, in his laws of motion, how rockets worked by 'action and reaction'. Exhaust gases shooting backwards pushed the rocket forwards.

Congreve's rockets

War rockets were noisy and frightening, but not so reliable as cannons. In India, Hyder Ali of Mysore used them in the late 1700s to fight the British, and from 1808 Sir William Congreve built rockets for the British army. Congreve's rockets had sticks 5 metres long for balance and were fired from metal tubes or A-shaped frames. They had a range of 1.8 kilometres. In the 1840s another British inventor, William Hale, replaced the useless weight of the rocket's stick with curved fins. These made army rockets fly further and faster.

Soldiers still preferred guns. Small rockets were useful at sea as distress signals, and were also fired to carry rescue lines from one ship to another. For most people, however, a rocket was just a firework; an exciting 'whoosh' of flame and sparks, vanishing in the night sky. The idea of controlled rocket flight, in space, seemed as far-fetched as science-fiction stories about 'men on the Moon'.

AD 1000	1241	c. 1500	1808	1820s	1821
BY THIS DATE CHINESE HAVE LEARNED HOW TO MAKE GUNPOWDER	TARTAR ARMY FIRES ROCKETS AT POLISH TROOPS	FIRST ATTEMPT AT ROCKET FLIGHT, IN CHINA, ENDS IN DISASTER	WILLIAM CONGREVE INVENTS HIS ARTILLERY ROCKET, WHICH IS FIRST TRIED AT SEA AGAINST THE FRENCH FLEET IN 1809	CLAUDIO RUGGIERI OF ITALY FIRES RATS AND MICE INTO THE AIR INSIDE ROCKETS	A ROCKET HARPOON GOES ON SALE

Telescope, before 1608

The telescope was invented during the late 1500s. By whom is not clear. In 1608, a Dutch spectacle-maker, Hans Lippershey, claimed to have put **lenses** together, to invent 'an instrument for seeing at a distance'. Other inventors, including his neighbour Zacharias Janssen, said they too had made telescopes. The Dutch government rejected Lippershey's claim to be the sole inventor – there were reports of earlier 'spyglasses' used by Italian soldiers. Within months, telescopes were being made and sold by lens-makers across Europe.

Star-gazing

Italy's greatest scientist, Galileo Galilei, heard about the new invention in 1609 while on a trip to Venice from his home in Padua. As soon as he got home, he ground his own lenses to make a telescope, which he turned skywards to gaze at the stars and planets.

Galileo was the first scientist to look at the Moon and planets through a telescope. What he saw changed people's ideas about the universe.

The Polish **astronomer** Nicolaus Copernicus had already challenged the ancient belief that the Earth was the centre of the universe. The telescope confirmed his theory about how the planets moved around the Sun. Galileo saw the **craters** on the Moon. He saw **sunspots**, too, and he discovered the four largest moons of Jupiter, **orbiting** the giant planet.

The lens for the eyepiece of Galileo's telescope was **concave**. The further, or object, lens was **convex**. In 1630, German astronomer Johannes Kepler made a better telescope, by fitting convex lenses for both the eyepiece and object lens. This gave a wider field of view and so was much better for looking into space.

Refractors and reflectors

Early telescopes worked by **refraction** (bending light), which caused blurring and distorted colours. In 1668 Sir Isaac Newton, the great British expert in light and **reflection** made the first reflecting telescope. It had a metal mirror to collect and focus the light. This solved the blurring and colour problems. Later, silvered glass mirrors were used. Today, aluminium is the usual material.

The first big astronomical telescopes were built in the late 1700s by British astronomer William Herschel. Even bigger ones were made by astronomers in the 1800s. The largest glass lens ever was made in 1897 for the world's biggest refracting telescope at the Yerkes Observatory in California, USA. It has a diameter of 1 metre.

Modern telescopes, like this one in Hawaii, are placed on high mountains. The dome slides open when the telescope inside is being used.

Today, city-based optical telescopes cannot get a clear view of the stars because of increasing air pollution. Most telescopes are now on mountain tops, such as Mauna Kea in Hawaii. This is the location for the world's biggest multi-mirror telescope, the Keck. The best site of all is in space, from where astronomers can get a cloudless view of millions of stars.

1609	1668	1781	1929	1948	1990
GALILEO GALILEI DISCOVERS JUPITER'S FOUR LARGEST MOONS WITH THE AID OF HIS TELESCOPE	SIR ISAAC NEWTON BUILDS THE FIRST REFLECTING TELESCOPE	WILLIAM HERSCHEL USES HIS TELESCOPE TO DISCOVER URANUS	BERNHARD SCHMIDT OF GERMANY INVENTS A SPECIAL TELESCOPE FOR PHOTOGRAPHING LARGE AREAS OF THE SKY	HALE REFLECTOR TELESCOPE AT MOUNT PALOMAR, CALIFORNIA, USA, HAS A 5-METRE MIRROR AND WEIGHS NEARLY 500 TONNES	FIRST BIG TELESCOPE IN SPACE – THE HUBBLE SPACE TELESCOPE

Liquid-fuelled rocket, 1926

After Galileo, **astronomers** remained at the forefront of space science until the 20th century. People could look into space, but they could not get there. Rockets burned a 'solid' fuel, **gunpowder**. A gunpowder rocket could only travel through air, because its fuel would not burn without **oxygen**. To fly into space, a rocket needed to take its own oxygen, in its fuel.

A Russian dreamer

The first person to suggest that a rocket burning liquid chemical mixtures that included oxygen could leave the Earth and travel into space was a Russian teacher, Konstantin Tsiolkovski. He spent years calculating how fast a rocket must go to escape from the Earth. He tested models in a wind tunnel he built himself, before publishing his idea – that a rocket firing in stages, one after the other, could break free of the Earth's **gravity** and reach space.

March 1926 and Robert H Goddard stands beside his rocket, the first to fly on liquid fuel, on his aunt's farm in Massachusetts, USA.

Tsiolkovski never built a rocket. Instead, his books and papers inspired a small band of other scientists in other countries, including the German Hermann Oberth and the American Robert Hutchings Goddard. Space travel was not taken seriously by most scientists – aeroplanes were still flimsy cloth-and-wire machines, only just able to cross oceans. Nor did generals welcome suggestions for long-range rocket **missiles**, put forward by Oberth to the German army during the First World War. Ignored by governments, the rocket scientists wrote to one another, swapping ideas.

Goddard's rockets

Robert H Goddard decided to test a rocket burning petroleum spirit and oxygen, a fuel which would burn even in airless space. In 1920 the *New York Times* newspaper made fun of his suggestion that rockets might one day fly to the Moon. 'How could a rocket fly in space' the newspaper article asked, 'without any air to push against?' It was a ridiculous notion. Not everyone thought so. In Germany, Hermann Oberth was writing about rockets travelling into space and visiting the planets.

In March 1926 Goddard tested his first rocket, nicknamed Nell, on his aunt's farm, with his wife taking notes. An assistant lit the rocket using a blow torch tied to a long stick! They watched in glee as the rocket shot up to a height of about sixty metres. Three years later Goddard launched a rocket carrying a camera, **barometer** and thermometer. In 1935 one of his rockets reached a height of over 2000 metres. Goddard had proved liquid-fuelled rockets worked.

Father of the US space programme

Robert H Goddard died in 1945, before the first American rocket had been fired into space, but he is rightly regarded as the pioneer of the US space programme. Born in 1882, he worked as a professor of physics, and spent his free time building rockets. His results were treated as 'cranky' in America. In Germany, however, scientists used Goddard's research to help build the *V-2* missile. In 1962 the Goddard Space Flight Center in Maryland, USA, was dedicated in Goddard's honour.

1903	1915	1923	1926	1931	1935
KONSTANTIN TSIOLKOVSKI PUBLISHES HIS ROCKET INTO SPACE THEORY. THE WRIGHT BROTHERS FLY A PLANE FOR THE FIRST TIME.	ROBERT H GODDARD INVENTS THE BAZOOKA, A ROCKET-FIRING WEAPON	HERMANN OBERTH WRITES A BOOK CALLED *THE ROCKET INTO INTERPLANETARY SPACE*	ROBERT H GODDARD TEST-FIRES THE WORLD'S FIRST LIQUID-FUELLED ROCKET	JOHANNES WINKLER OF GERMANY BUILDS A ROCKET FUELLED BY METHANE AND OXYGEN	A 'GODDARD ROCKET' FLIES FASTER THAN SOUND

Radio telescope, 1937

By 1900 scientists were beginning to realize just how big space was. They used optical telescopes to look at visible stars. They knew too, of other invisible forms of **radiation** given off by stars, including radio waves, X-rays and infra-red rays. New 'radio' telescopes that could detect and study these rays told scientists much about the size and age of the universe.

Scientists became aware of radiation in space in the late 1880s, when inventors such as Heinrich Hertz of Germany began studying radio waves. Work on radio by the Italian engineer Guglielmo Marconi led to the first radio broadcasts in the early 1900s.

Listening to the crackle of radio signals, engineers came across a puzzle. From time to time, they picked up unusual signals, with no known source. Where could these mysterious radio signals be coming from?

Karl Jansky went to work for the Bell Telephone company in 1928. Three years later he traced radio signals from the stars.

Signals from space

Radio signals from space were finally identified in 1931. An American engineer named Karl Jansky was working for Bell Laboratories in the United States. His job was to trace mysterious radio signals which interfered with short-wave radio telephone calls to ships at sea. He built a receiver to 'listen in', and detected one whistling signal that he picked up four minutes earlier each day. This time-shift coincided with the reappearance of stars. It gave him the clue he needed to track the signal to the star-system Sagittarius, millions of kilometres away. Jansky's discovery caused a sensation, but he was not an **astronomer** and never followed up his breakthrough.

The first radio telescope was made in 1937 by Grote Reber, a Chicago-based astronomer who set up the device in his backyard. Reber was a '**radio ham**', and spent most of his spare time and money on his hobby. He set up a dish **antenna** measuring 3 metres across and after two years of trying, managed to receive signals from stars. He set to work drawing a 'radio map' of the Milky Way **galaxy**, which he published in 1944.

By the 1950s astronomers, such as Britain's Sir Bernard Lovell, had realized the importance of radio astronomy, and the first big radio telescopes were built. In 1957 the Jodrell Bank dish tracked the world's first artificial satellite, *Sputnik 1*.

There are 27 mobile dishes on rails in the Y-shaped Very Large Array radio telescope, set up west of Socorro in New Mexico, USA.

Looking for life

One of the most intriguing tasks taken on by radio astronomers was to look for signs of life in outer space. The Search for Extraterrestrial Intelligence (SETI) programme was set up, to listen for radio signals from other worlds, and to send signals from Earth to distant stars. The giant 305-metre Arecibo radio telescope in Puerto Rico has beamed signals towards stars 250,000 **light years** away. It will be 50,000 years before any answer comes back!

1904	1937	1957	1960s	1974	1980
CHRISTIAN HULSMEYER PATENTS A 'RADIO DETECTOR'	GROTE REBER BUILDS THE FIRST WORKING RADIO TELESCOPE	JODRELL BANK IN ENGLAND IS THE WORLD'S FIRST BIG RADIO TELESCOPE, DESIGNED BY BERNARD LOVELL	RADIO ASTRONOMERS DISCOVER QUASARS – THE MOST DISTANT OBJECTS DETECTED FROM EARTH	THE RADIO TELESCOPE AT ARECIBO, PUERTO RICO, IS MADE OF OVER 38,000 SHEETS OF ALUMINIUM COVERING A HOLLOW IN THE GROUND	THE VERY LARGE ARRAY IN THE USA IS THE WORLD'S MOST POWERFUL RADIO TELESCOPE

Satellite, 1957

In the 1660s, Sir Isaac Newton described **gravity** – the force that keeps the Moon (a natural satellite) **orbiting** the Earth. By the 1930s scientists such as rocket pioneer Hermann Oberth were trying to work out how to send artificial 'moons' into space. They calculated that a rocket reaching a speed of about eleven kilometres per second would break away from the pull of the Earth and go into orbit, becoming a satellite – a miniature moon. Such satellites could have many uses for communications, for studying space and for looking down on the Earth.

Passers-by stare at a model of Sputnik 1, the first artificial satellite. Its launch by the Soviet Union in 1957 made news headlines around the world.

The Soviets launch Sputnik

Launching a satellite needed a big rocket. Before 1957, research rockets had reached only the fringes of space. To launch a satellite, a more powerful, three-stage **step rocket** was needed. As the first and second stages used up their fuel, they separated and fell back to the ground, leaving the final stage to speed on into orbit.

During the 1950s, the **Soviet Union** secretly built very large **missiles** to carry **nuclear weapons**. From these missiles, Soviet rocket-builders developed the 300-tonne *Vostok* satellite launcher, designed by aircraft engineer Sergei Korolev. On 4 October 1957, this rocket launched a 61-centimetre sphere, named *Sputnik* (Companion) into orbit. The world's first artificial satellite weighed 83 kilograms and as it circled the Earth, its 'bleep' signals were heard by radio listeners all over the world. A month later, a second Soviet satellite, *Sputnik 2*, ten times heavier, carried the first animal into space – a dog named Laika.

The space race

The Americans had also been building rockets, such as the *Aerobee* designed by James Van Allen. The Soviet Union's success was an enormous shock to the US government. The Americans' own satellite programme had been held up by rivalry between the army and the air force, each of which had their own missiles. The Americans had pinned their hopes on a much smaller scientific rocket named *Vanguard*, but it was having problems. Suddenly, they found themselves in a space race with the Soviets.

A US military rocket, the *Jupiter*, was hurriedly modified to launch *Explorer*, the first US satellite, in 1958. The first *Explorer* satellites were designed by Van Allen and his team, and the doughnut-shaped radiation zones they discovered were named the Van Allen Belts.

Later, other countries launched satellites. France was the third nation to do so, followed by China, Japan and Britain. Some satellites stay in orbit for many years. Others, closer to the Earth, burn up as they re-enter the atmosphere. The biggest satellite ever recovered from space was the *LDF* (*Long Duration Exposure Facility*), a bus-sized capsule launched by the USA in 1984 and picked up by the Space Shuttle *Columbia* in 1990.

1946	1957	1958	1958	1958	1958
JAMES VAN ALLEN WORKS ON GERMAN V-2 ROCKETS AND DEVELOPS *AEROBEE* RESEARCH ROCKET	SOVIET LAUNCHES OF *SPUTNIK 1* AND *SPUTNIK 2* STARTLE SCIENTIFIC WORLD	*EXPLORER 1*, FIRST US SATELLITE, LAUNCHED BY A *JUPITER C* ROCKET. IT BURNS UP IN 1970 AFTER 58,376 ORBITS.	US *VANGUARD* ROCKET LAUNCHES ITS FIRST SATELLITE, WHICH DISCOVERS THE INNER LAYER OF THE VAN ALLEN RADIATION BELTS	SOVIET'S *SPUTNIK 3* IS FIRST MULTI-PURPOSE SATELLITE, WITH AN ARRAY OF SCIENTIFIC INSTRUMENTS	US GOVERNMENT SETS UP **NATIONAL AERONAUTICS AND SPACE ADMINISTRATION (NASA)**

Space probe, 1959

A satellite is held in **orbit** by the Earth's **gravity**. To break free of the Earth and become a space probe, travelling out to the Moon or the planets, a spacecraft must reach '**escape velocity**' – roughly forty thousand kilometres per hour. The **Soviet Union** led the way with *Luna 1* in 1959. The first probe to escape the Earth, it sent radio signals from 597,000 kilometres away. Six months later, *Luna 2* hit the Moon.

Building a probe

In the 1950s computers were so big they filled rooms, and cameras and radios were heavy. The invention of the **integrated circuit** by Jack Kilby in 1958 meant that onboard electronic equipment could be made very small. A rocket could send a small, but electronically 'smart' probe zooming out across space to explore the planets.

The space and arms race drove the Soviet Union and the United States to spend huge amounts of money inventing electronic guidance systems and smaller, more powerful computers. Calculating the course a tiny space craft should take on a journey lasting several years was very complicated! The target planet is moving and so is the Earth – the launch pad – so the probe has to be sent on a curving path. By the end of the 1960s the United States had taken a vital lead in space **electronics**.

*The Soviet Luna 2 probe made history, and a new **crater**, in 1959 when it crashed into the Moon.*

Alone in space

A space probe had to be as near-perfect as human engineers could make it. Every system had a back-up in case something went wrong. The probe had to work for many months alone in space. It had to carry its own power supply in the form of specially made batteries, solar cells or nuclear reactors. It had to be tough enough to stand the shock of acceleration during launch. It also had to survive in the hostile environment of space.

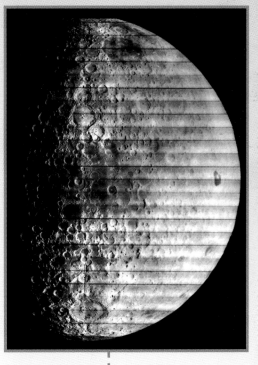

A space probe did not need a streamlined shape, like a jet plane, since there is no **friction** in space. It could have bits sticking out all over – for example, solar panels and radio dishes and aerials. Engineers fitted electronic guidance systems, **gyroscopes** to detect changes in acceleration, and small gas jets or rockets to make steering changes. They installed cameras to photograph the planets and instruments such as **radiation** detectors, thermometers and **spectroscopes** to record changing conditions around the probe.

1960s probes sent back the first pictures of the far side of the Moon. Each complete image was built in strips.

Probes to the planets

The United States and the Soviet Union sent robot probes to the planets Venus and Mars, beginning with *Venera 3* which hit Venus in 1965. **NASA** scientists such as Carl Sagan planned trips to Mars and across the **solar system**. Such journeys across millions of kilometres take many years. *Pioneer 10* left the solar system in 1983, eleven years after leaving Earth. The *Voyager 2* probe, launched by the Americans in 1977, visited Jupiter in 1979, Saturn in 1981, Uranus in 1986, and Neptune in 1989. This amazing space explorer is expected to remain 'alive' until 2020, periodically sending back data from far beyond the solar system.

1959	1965	1970	1977	1989-1993	1999
THE SOVIET PROBE *LUNA 1* FLIES INTO SPACE BEYOND EARTH-ORBIT	US *MARINER 4* PROBE SENDS BACK PHOTOGRAPHS OF MARS	THE SOVIET UNION'S *VENERA 7* IS FIRST PROBE TO SURVIVE LANDING ON VENUS	*VOYAGER 1* AND *VOYAGER 2* LEAVE EARTH, CARRYING MESSAGES FROM EARTH FOR ANY ALIENS WHO MIGHT FIND THEM	NASA'S *MAGELLAN* PROBE MAPS SURFACE OF VENUS BY **RADAR**	*GALILEO* PROBE ORBITS JUPITER, STUDYING ITS FOUR LARGEST MOONS

Weather and resources satellites, 1960

Scientists quickly realized that a satellite in **orbit** could be the perfect 'weather station' in space. A satellite could photograph land and sea, giving up-to-the-minute information about crops, drought and pollution. It could even search for oil or gas hidden beneath the ground.

The first aerial photographs were taken from balloons and aeroplanes. The first weather satellite was launched in 1960 and today the world is ringed by satellites, watching the weather and warning of looming environmental problems.

Eyes in the sky

Scientists were delighted with the first satellite photographs of Earth, sent back in 1958. No one could now argue that the world was flat! Satellites revealed that the Earth is pear-shaped. By 1959 satellites were sending back television pictures showing the clouds, oceans and continents, and the first weather satellite was being built.

Satellites track hurricanes, whirling across the ocean, and early warning gives people on land time to flee or seek shelter from the storm.

Today we see satellite weather photos on television, but before 1960 almost all weather information came from ground stations and scattered weather ships at sea. The first weather satellite was called *Tiros* (*Television and Infra-Red Observation Satellite*) and was launched in 1960. It took one photo an hour from a height of 750 kilometres. Thousands of photographs were sent back to weather

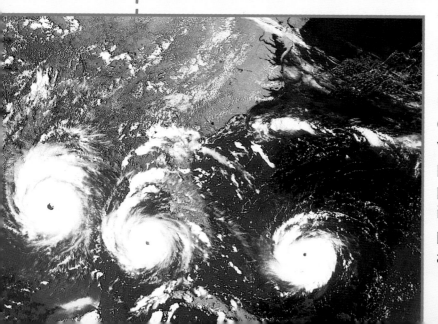

stations on Earth from ten *Tiros* satellites. In the 1970s bigger *Nimbus* satellites took over. Weather satellites in **geostationary orbit** observe weather patterns, while others fly over the poles, so that the whole planet is covered. Their data is analysed by computers to predict the weather more accurately than ever before.

A technician checks Tiros 1, *the first US weather satellite, launched in 1960 and the first of a series of weather satellites.*

With the satellites on watch, hurricanes can be spotted as they form over the ocean, giving time for people in the storm's path to flee and seek shelter.

Earth resource satellites

Scientific Earth-watch satellites, such as *OGO-1* (*Orbiting Geophysical Observatory* – launched in 1964), were placed in geostationary orbit. Using **radar**, television and special cameras, such satellites gave scientists a clearer picture of human use, and misuse, of the planet's resources.

Landsat 1, launched in 1972, was the first satellite to send back data about farming, forestry, minerals, land use and water resources. Other Landsats have found new reserves of petroleum, tracked pollution of rivers and lakes, monitored city growth, and warned of floods or droughts. *Seasat* in 1978 and *Geosat* in 1985 used radar to map the ocean and the ocean floor.

1959	1959	1960	1964	1965	1972
USA'S *VANGUARD 2* SATELLITE TAKES FIRST PHOTOGRAPHS OF CLOUDS COVERING EARTH	*EXPLORER 6* SENDS BACK FIRST TV PICTURES OF EARTH	*TIROS 1* IS FIRST WEATHER SATELLITE	*OGO-1* IS FIRST ORBITING GEOPHYSICAL OBSERVATORY	*TIROS 10*, FUNDED BY US WEATHER BUREAU, HAS TWO TELEVISION CAMERAS TO SCAN EARTH'S WEATHER	*LANDSAT* IS FIRST EARTH-RESOURCES SATELLITE

Spy and navigation satellites, 1960

The first satellite-launchers were rockets originally designed to carry **nuclear weapons**. During the **Cold War** of the 1950s and 60s, the United States and the **Soviet Union** spent vast sums of money on new weapons. This arms race also sparked off rivalry in space. Both sides launched secret satellites to spy from space and as navigation beacons to guide their submarines and aircraft.

Spies in space

During the Cold War the Soviet Union kept almost all its space research secret. The United States was more open, allowing press and television coverage of most space-flights, except the secret military missions. The secret spacecraft had cameras and **radar** that could detect very small targets. They were placed in **orbits** that took them over enemy territory to spy on military bases, rocket launch sites and research centres.

Discoverer 13 returned to Earth in 1960 – the first satellite to be recovered from orbit, with its data and photos.

Modern spy satellites such as the US *Crystals* check that **disarmament** agreements are being properly carried out. So sensitive are their 'electronic eyes' (infra-red telescopes and heat-seeking equipment) that they can send back images of objects as small as trees or trucks. Electronic 'ferret' satellites can eavesdrop on radio and telephone calls. The US government has plans for a **missile** defence screen, using satellites and rockets to shoot down enemy missiles.

Navigation satellites

Since ships first sailed the oceans over 5000 years ago, people have found their way by looking at the stars. With the space age beginning in 1957, the satellite became an artificial star, which could be tracked from the ground. Navigation satellites can now guide a ship, a plane, or even a truck in the desert.

In 1960, the US Navy launched *Transit*, a secret satellite beacon, to guide its nuclear submarines. By 1964 there were seven *Transit* satellites orbiting the Earth. Radio signals from the satellites are picked up by computerized receivers on ships and submarines.

A later system, developed in the 1990s by the US Air Force, is the *Navstar* Global Positioning System (GPS). It uses 21 satellites plus spares. To find its position, a truck or a ship uses its radio and computer equipment to locate four satellites in space. The computer uses this data to pinpoint its position exactly on the surface – or even under water.

Inventing the electronic eye

In 1969 two American **electronics** engineers, Willard Boyle and George Smith, invented in less than two hours a gadget called a charge-coupled device (CCD). It is a chip with a grid containing millions of microscopic light-sensitive pixels, which convert light into electrical signals. **NASA** took up the idea to develop smaller cameras for space use, and the CCD became the electronic eye in spy satellites and the Hubble Space Telescope. Its invention led to the development of digital cameras in the 1990s.

How GPS satellites work

A ship in the middle of an ocean can find its position by linking to four navigation satellites orbiting in space.

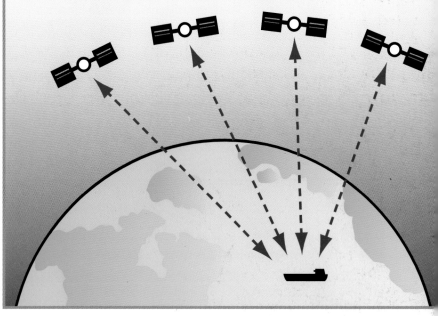

1896	1960	1961	1978	1983	1995
FIRST SHIP-TO-SHORE RADIO SIGNALS, SENT BY GUGLIELMO MARCONI	US NAVY LAUNCHES FIRST *TRANSIT* NAVIGATION SATELLITE	US *MIDAS 1* IS FIRST SPY SATELLITE ABLE TO SPOT MISSILE LAUNCHES	US LAUNCHES FIRST *NAVSTAR* SATELLITE	US STRATEGIC DEFENCE INITIATIVE, OR 'STAR WARS', SYSTEM IS PROPOSED TO TRACK AND SHOOT DOWN ENEMY MISSILES IN SPACE	US AIR FORCE'S *NAVSTAR* GLOBAL POSITIONING SYSTEM FULLY OPERATIONAL

The first satellite, *Sputnik 1,* showed that it was possible to send craft into space. In 1960 the Soviets launched a craft carrying two dogs and brought them back safely after 20 hours in space. This showed three things. One, Soviet rockets were powerful enough to launch a human-weight **payload**. Two, Soviet engineers had mastered the tricky manoeuvres of re-entry and landing. Three, their spacecraft had a life-support system able to keep living things alive in space.

Cosmonauts and astronauts

Space-flight was presumed to be very demanding, physically and mentally. The **Soviet Union** and United States had been training space-fliers since the late 1950s, picking young and fit pilots. It was a jet pilot, Yuri Gagarin, who rocketed into history on 12 April 1961. He was the Soviet Union's first **cosmonaut**. In an historic first he circled the Earth once, in 108 minutes. His brief trip, strapped into his seat inside the cramped *Vostok* capsule, ended with a parachute landing and a hero's welcome. Future flights were planned for Gagarin, but he was killed in a plane crash in 1968.

The Americans picked seven pilots to be their first **astronauts**. There were no women among them. In the late 1950s there were very few women jet pilots, and many doctors thought the stresses of space-flight would be too severe for a female astronaut. In 1963, Valentina Tereshkova of the Soviet Union proved this was not so, and since her flight women have made many space-flights.

*Two dogs named Strelka and Belka were the first animals to return from **orbiting** the Earth, in* Sputnik 5. *They landed safely by parachute.*

Success and tragedy in space

The Americans' first manned craft was the cone-shaped *Mercury* capsule, just big enough for one person. The Soviet *Vostok* was three times heavier, and by 1964 the *Voskhod 1* had put three cosmonauts into space together. In 1965 a Soviet cosmonaut made the first space walk.

The dangers of space-flight were shown two years later, however, when the new *Soyuz* spacecraft suffered a fatal accident in 1967. Soviet cosmonaut Vladimir Komarov died when the re-entry system failed. His landing capsule survived the crash to the ground, but he was killed.

The Americans moved on to two-man *Gemini* missions, involving the **docking** of two craft in space. US astronauts perfected re-entry and landing techniques, using parachutes to 'splash down' into the ocean. Much of this success was due to the work of Robert Gilruth, boss of the Manned Spacecraft Center at Houston, Texas. The Gemini programme led on to the bigger *Apollo* craft. *Apollo 8* flew round the Moon in 1968 and *Apollo 11* landed on the Moon in 1969.

Yuri Gagarin strapped into the cramped cabin of the Vostok spacecraft, circling the Earth in 1961. His brief flight turned fantasy into reality – the journey into space had begun – and made Gagarin a world hero, though he never flew in space again.

Robert Gilruth (1913–2000)

Like many space pioneers, American Robert Gilruth began as an aircraft engineer. In the 1940s he worked on **robot** planes, **missiles** and rocket planes that flew faster than sound. In 1958 he was asked to head the team of scientists at **NASA**, who built the *Gemini* and *Apollo* spacecraft. Gilruth had a knack for picking the right people, and the triumphant *Apollo* Moon flights were a testament to the success of his team's work.

1961	1962	1963	1967	1981	1998
YURI GAGARIN MAKES FIRST MANNED SPACE-FLIGHT	JOHN GLENN IS FIRST US ASTRONAUT TO ORBIT EARTH	SOVIET COSMONAUT VALENTINA TERESHKOVA IS FIRST WOMAN IN SPACE	VLADIMIR KOMAROV IS FIRST PERSON TO BE KILLED IN SPACE	FIRST FLIGHT OF US SHUTTLE, CAPABLE OF TAKING SEVEN ASTRONAUTS INTO SPACE	JOHN GLENN RETURNS TO SPACE, BECOMING WORLD'S OLDEST SHUTTLE PASSENGER AT THE AGE OF 77

Spacesuit, 1961

Illustrations to science-fiction stories of the 1800s showed Moon explorers wearing everyday clothes. By the 1930s, artists were drawing spacemen in spacesuits, for by then scientists had realized that no human could live in space without the protection of special clothing. The modern spacesuit has come through several stages of design, with engineers, doctors and the **astronauts** themselves all working together.

Suits under water and in the air

The first 'spacesuits' were deep-sea diving suits, invented in the 1800s. These were airtight, as well as waterproof, with a metal helmet. They were supplied with air through hoses. In the 1930s, the first 'pressure suits' were worn by high-altitude pilots and balloonists. Above 20,000 metres, pilots must wear pressure suits to keep the fluids in their bodies moving. In the late 1940s the first supersonic pilots, such as the American, Chuck Yeager, risked becoming unconscious if they flew without pressure suits. When the human body is stressed by rapid acceleration, the supply of blood to the brain may be slowed down or cut off.

In the 1960s US test pilots flew the X-15 rocket plane so fast and so high they needed to wear pressure suits, like astronauts.

Life support in space

The first person to wear a spacesuit in space was Soviet **cosmonaut** Yuri Gagarin in 1961, although he never left the safety of his cabin. Not until 1965 did people venture outside a spacecraft, floating in space with only a spacesuit for protection. The first suits were not very different from air force flying suits and were not easy to move in. The Moon suits developed by **NASA** designers for the *Apollo* astronauts between 1969 and 1972 were more comfortable, with rubber joints for walking and bending. The suits were liquid-cooled. They were made of layers of nylon and other synthetic materials, and had a tough outer layer of teflon-coated glass fibre.

Shuttle suits

Since the 1980s, designers have developed new clothing for astronauts working on space stations or crewing the Space Shuttles. Inside, crews usually work in shirts and trousers. Outside the spacecraft, an astronaut must wear a spacesuit.

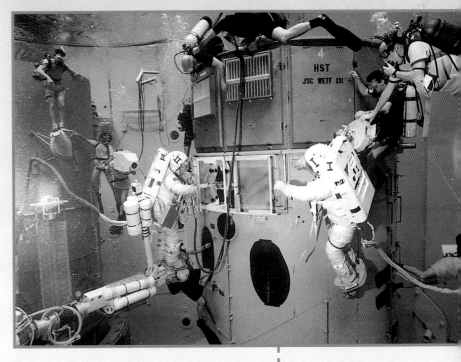

The spacesuit's life-support system supplies them with pure **oxygen** to breathe. On Earth we breathe a mixture of nitrogen and oxygen. The suit has several layers to protect the wearer from **radiation** and to prevent the suit being punctured by flying dust particles. The suits are reusable and come in interchangeable parts, made in different sizes, so they can be assembled for each mission to fit men and women astronauts.

To train for space-walks, astronauts in spacesuits practised under water in giant tanks. Floating felt very like zero-gravity.

On the chest is a control pad and toolkit. The inner suit has heating elements to keep the wearer warm and water-filled tubes to keep him or her cool in the full sun. The helmet's gold-tinted visor is scratch-resistant and shades the eyes from the blinding sunlight. Underneath, the astronaut wears the 'Snoopy cap' containing a personal radio. The suit comes with a built-in waste-disposal system, in case the wearer needs to go to the toilet. Though heavier than the astronaut on the ground, it is feather-light in the weightlessness of space.

1930s	1947	1961	1965	1969	1971
PRESSURE SUITS TESTED BY PIONEER HIGH FLIERS IN PLANES AND BALLOONS	FIRST SUPERSONIC FLIGHT, BY CHUCK YEAGER OF THE USA IN THE BELL *X-1* ROCKET PLANE	FIRST PERSON IN SPACE, WEARING A SPACESUIT ALL THE TIME – YURI GAGARIN OF THE **SOVIET UNION**	SOVIET COSMONAUT ALEKSEI LEONOV IS FIRST 'SPACE WALKER'	USA'S *APOLLO* ASTRONAUTS WALK AND WORK ON THE MOON, PROTECTED BY THEIR SPACESUITS	AMERICAN CAR RACER RICHARD PETTY WEARS A WATER-COOLED SUIT, BASED ON SPACESUIT TECHNOLOGY

Moon rocket, 1969

The giant Moon rocket that took the first **astronauts** to the Moon in 1969 was a direct development of Second World War **missiles**, designed to bomb cities. The inventive brain behind the American *Saturn 5* Moon rocket belonged to German engineer Wernher von Braun. As a young rocket-builder in the 1930s, von Braun dreamed of giant space rockets. In 1934 he designed the *A-2*, a rocket fuelled by ethyl alcohol and liquid **oxygen**.

A Saturn 5 launch, as the first stage engines lift it slowly off the ground.

The V-2 missile

When the Second World War began in 1939, von Braun went to work at the top-secret rocket research base at Peenemünde in northern Germany. His team built the *A-4* rocket in 1942, which flew at five times the speed of sound and soared to the edge of space. Renamed the *V-2*, this rocket became a deadly weapon, hurtling down on Belgian and British cities without warning. Fortunately, the new terror weapon came too late to prevent Germany's defeat. By 1945 Peenemünde had been destroyed by bombing, but many German scientists, plans and rocket parts were seized by the Allies.

Building the Moon rocket

Von Braun went to the United States, and began designing new rockets based on the *V-2*. Some were army missiles, but von Braun wanted to build space rockets, big enough to send spacecraft into **orbit** around the Earth, and to the Moon and back.

Von Braun helped launch the first US satellite in 1958, but realized that the Russians had a big lead in the space race. US President John F Kennedy vowed that the nation would land men on the Moon before the 1960s ended – a huge challenge for von Braun and the other **NASA** engineers. At great speed, they built the biggest rocket in the world – the *Saturn 5*.

The *Saturn 5* had eleven separate engines in three stages, weighed 2.7 million kilograms and was over 110 metres tall. The ground shook as it lifted from the launch pad, burning over 2 million litres of fuel in the first 2.5 minutes of flight. It sent six spacecraft to the Moon between 1969 and 1972, and also launched the US space laboratory, *Skylab*.

Successors to Saturn

When the *Apollo* and *Skylab* programmes ended in 1973, the giant rocket became a museum exhibit. NASA turned its attention to the reusable Space Shuttle in 1981. Big rockets are still used for satellite launches. Modern ones include the US *Atlas* and *Delta* launchers, China's *Long March* rocket, and the European Space Agency's *Ariane*.

Wernher von Braun (1912–1977)

Wernher von Braun was born in Wirsitz, Germany (now part of Poland). He read Hermann Oberth's book *The Rocket Into Interplanetary Space*, and later built small model rockets. During the Second World War, von Braun and General Walter Dornberger were put in charge of the rocket plant at Peenemünde. When the war ended, von Braun went to the United States, and in 1955 he became a US citizen. The 1969 *Apollo 11* mission saw his dream come true – sending people to the Moon. Von Braun left NASA in 1972 and died in 1977.

1944	1949	1958	1969	1973	1979
GERMAN V-2 ROCKETS FIRED AGAINST ANTWERP AND LONDON	US *VIKING* LAUNCHER IS AN IMPROVED VERSION OF THE *V-2*	FIRST US SATELLITE, *EXPLORER 1*, LAUNCHED BY A *JUPITER* ROCKET	A *SATURN 5* ROCKET SENDS *APOLLO 11* SPACECRAFT TO THE MOON. THE **SOVIET UNION'S** *N-1* MOON ROCKET BLOWS UP	*SATURN 5* ROCKET LAUNCHES USA'S *SKYLAB* SPACE STATION	FIRST TEST LAUNCH OF EUROPEAN SPACE AGENCY'S *ARIANE* ROCKET

Moon lander, 1969

Every space explorer looked towards the Moon. The Americans spent billions of dollars building a craft able to land people on the Moon and return them to Earth. They made it in 1969. When **astronauts** will return to the Moon, no one knows.

The Moon race

The Soviet probe *Luna 2* crashed onto the Moon in September 1959. A month later *Luna 3* took the first photographs of the far side of the Moon. Because of its **rotation**, the Moon always shows the same side to people on Earth.

By 1960 **NASA** engineers were planning to build the huge *Saturn 5* rocket to send a three-man craft from the Earth to the Moon. Most Americans believed they were in a race with the **Soviet Union** to put people on the Moon. Hundreds of companies were involved in the project, making thousands of components – fuel cells, **electronics**, cameras, life-support systems, engines, spacesuits. Every part had to be tested hundreds of times – one failure, and three astronauts would be stranded in space.

Neil Armstrong and Edwin 'Buzz' Aldrin were the first people to walk on the Moon. They carried out many experiments such as this one, to measure seismic ('moonquake') activity, during their lunar landing.

To seek suitable landing sites, unmanned craft were sent to the Moon. The US *Ranger* craft was launched in 1964 and 1965 to send back close-up pictures. In 1966 the Soviet *Luna 9* made the first **soft-landing** on the Moon and sent back the first television pictures. To test landing techniques, the Americans landed *Surveyor 3* on the Moon in 1967. *Lunar Orbiters* circled the Moon, descending to heights of 45 kilometres to photograph possible landing sites.

The Apollo Moon mission

Thousands of people worked on the *Apollo* craft. It had three sections. The command **module** was the control centre and living quarters and the only part to return to Earth. The service module contained rocket engines and fuel. The lunar module was the only part intended to land on the Moon. It looked flimsy, with its spidery legs and paper-thin metal skin. It was only meant for two people – the third crewman would remain inside the **orbiting** command module.

The *Apollo* programme suffered a terrible setback in 1967 when fire killed three astronauts on the ground. The first manned *Apollo* flight did not take place until October 1968. Just two months later three astronauts flew around the Moon in *Apollo 8*. In March 1969 *Apollo 9* tested the lunar module in Earth's orbit. Next, in May 1969, came a practice run for a Moon landing, as *Apollo 10* orbited the Moon, dropping to 14.5 kilometres above the surface, but not landing. In July 1969, *Apollo 11* repeated the performance. This time the lunar module landed, and for the first time people walked on the surface of the Moon.

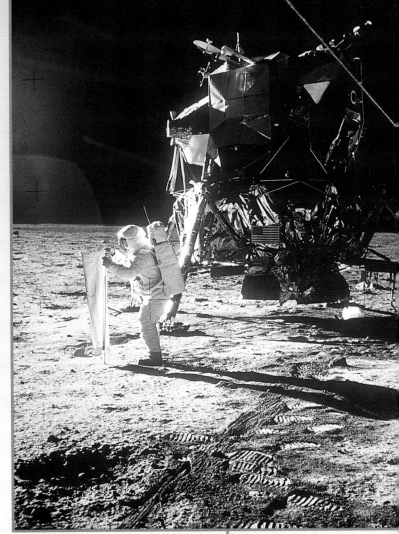

The flag set on the Moon by the Apollo *11 crew, and their footprints, were not disturbed by any movement on the airless, weatherless Moon.*

1850s	1959	1961	1968	1969	1972
FIRST PHOTOGRAPHS OF THE MOON TAKEN FROM EARTH	THE SOVIET UNION'S *LUNA 2* IS THE FIRST PROBE TO HIT THE MOON	PRESIDENT KENNEDY PROMISES TO LAND AMERICANS ON THE MOON BEFORE THE DECADE IS OVER	*APOLLO 8* FLIES AROUND THE MOON AND RETURNS SAFELY TO EARTH	*APOLLO 11* ASTRONAUTS NEIL ARMSTRONG AND EDWIN 'BUZZ' ALDRIN LAND ON THE MOON	*APOLLO 17* IS LAST APOLLO MOON MISSION

Space rover, 1970

Many scientists argued against sending men to the Moon. Send machines instead, they said. Machines don't need air or food. Space rovers did go to the Moon and to Mars. They showed that many useful scientific experiments can be done by **robot** machines, programmed by computer and controlled by radio from Earth.

Robots and rovers on the Moon

Robot explorers were first tried on the Moon in 1970. The Soviet *Luna 16* craft landed on the Moon and from it emerged an eight-wheeled vehicle – the first robot to explore the Moon. Known as *Lunokhod*, the solar-powered robot carried television cameras and a small X-ray telescope. It could use its remotely controlled arms to examine rocks. It rolled a total distance of over 10 kilometres during a five-month mission, surviving the freezing cold of the lunar night that was fourteen Earth-days long.

The lunar rover had four-wheel drive and could reach speeds of 11 kilometres an hour. Astronauts could use the rover to carry equipment over the Moon.

On the last three US Moon landings (*Apollos 15, 16* and *17*), the **astronauts** 'unfolded' the remarkable lunar rover. This electric car trundled about at a top speed of 14 kilometres per hour and carried twice its own weight. The average car carries only half its weight. The four-wheel drive of the Moon-buggy used a new lubricant system invented by air force engineer John B Christian. It kept the wheels turning smoothly in any temperature from freezing cold to scorching hot. The buggy was steered by a T-shaped controller, not a steering wheel. Riding allowed the astronauts to explore more of the Moon and save precious **oxygen** and water.

Robots on Mars

A manned flight to Mars and back will be long and difficult, but robots have already begun to explore the red planet. In 1997 the *Pathfinder* spacecraft released the small *Sojourner* vehicle, the first rover to move about another planet. It weighed about 4 kilograms on Mars and crawled at 60 centimetres a minute, never straying further than 10 metres from its parent lander. *Sojourner* had six wheels to make climbing easier and a solar panel for electric power. It kept working for three months until its parent craft got too cold and 'died'.

In 2003 **NASA** plans to launch the *Mars Exploration Rover*. Two probes will parachute down to a bouncy, airbag-cushioned landing on Mars and release two robot rovers, Each rover will cover 100 metres during a Martian day – just over 24 hours.

The little Sojourner *robot rolled up to examine rocks near the* Pathfinder *lander. It found evidence of water long ago on Mars.*

The first Moon drivers

The first people to drive on another world were US astronauts David Scott and James Irwin in July 1971. Their twelve-day *Apollo 15* mission included two excursions in the lunar rover, which at first proved hard to steer – a 'real bucking bronco' – in the Moon's one-sixth **gravity**. They needed their seatbelts! Both astronauts fell over while exploring on foot, but found that the improved spacesuits they were wearing made getting up easier.

1969	1970	1971	1972	1997
FIRST ALSEP SCIENTIFIC PACKAGE LEFT ON MOON BY *APOLLO 12*, WITH A NUCLEAR-POWERED BATTERY TO KEEP THE EXPERIMENTS WORKING FOR A YEAR	*LUNOKHOD* IS FIRST ROBOT EXPLORER ON THE MOON	*APOLLO 15* LANDS FIRST OF THREE LUNAR ROVERS	THIRD AND LAST LUNAR ROVER IS LEFT ON MOON	*PATHFINDER'S SOJOURNER* ROBOT CRAWLS ON MARS, STUDYING ROCKS

Space food and fitness, 1971

The first **astronauts** were all young, fit pilots. Today's space travellers enjoy greater comfort, and do not undergo such strenuous training. Special food and advances in space medicine make sure that astronauts stay healthy while in space.

In 1961, Yuri Gagarin spent less than two hours in space, and did not eat, wash or sleep. As humans made longer flights, lasting up to a year, scientists had to solve the 'housekeeping' and fitness problems caused by long stays in space. The launch of the **Soviet Union's** space station *Salyut* in 1971 began the new era of making space-flight safer and more comfortable.

Eating in space

Eating and drinking are a welcome, and sometimes amusing, part of daily routine for astronauts on long stays in space.

Because everything is weightless in space, eating and drinking present problems. Liquid floats out of a cup and crumbs float around a cabin. Food trays and cutlery would float around too, unless held in place by suckers, magnets or sticky strips.

Freeze-dried food was invented by E W Flosdorff in 1947. At first it was just coffee and orange juice. Most space food goes into space frozen or dried, and is defrosted or **rehydrated** before eating. Drinks are usually squirted into the mouth or sipped through straws.

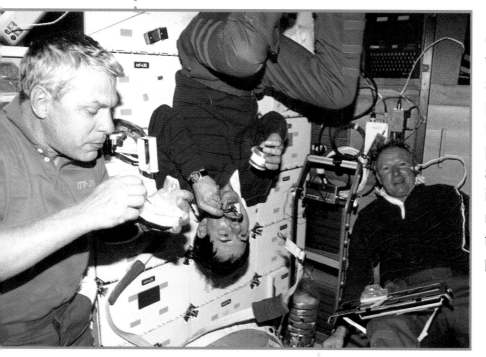

Following the example of airlines, which started serving pre-cooked, previously frozen meals in 1945, space planners know that appetizing meals are important for crew morale. Menus are therefore carefully planned.

On a typical working day in space, shuttle astronauts breakfast on orange juice and scrambled eggs. Lunch might be soup, a sandwich and a banana. Dinner at the end of the working day might be steak, vegetables and a pudding.

Health and hygiene

To sleep, astronauts zip themselves into sleeping bags. Velcro, invented by Swiss engineer Georges de Mestral in 1957, is useful for keeping things stuck down. For extra warmth, astronauts have blankets of metal foil, so effective that it is also used to wrap premature babies.

Washing is tricky in weightlessness – water is too precious to be allowed to fly about the spacecraft. Astronauts can take a shower inside a sealed unit. The space shower, which reuses or recycles 93 per cent of water, was invented by **NASA** engineer Russell Garcia. Toilets are vacuum-operated, to suck away the waste – no flushing in space!

About half of all astronauts suffer from space sickness. Mae Jemison, the first black American woman in space, studied motion sickness in zero gravity. She found that meditation techniques helped. Colds can also be a problem – a runny nose is no joke when you are weightless. Better diets and medicines help keep astronauts fit, and they exercise every day on machines to make their muscles work. Without gravity, muscles have nothing to push and pull against, and so begin to waste away after weeks in space. Bones too become weaker, because of calcium loss. Some of the first astronauts could hardly stand when they landed back on Earth.

1961	1963	1971	1985	1987	1987
YURI GAGARIN PROVES THAT A HUMAN CAN SURVIVE SPACE-FLIGHT	VALENTINA TERESHKOVA IS FIRST WOMAN IN SPACE	SOVIET *SALYUT* IS FIRST SPACE STATION, WITH A REFRIGERATOR AND 90 DAYS' DRINKING WATER STORED IN RUBBER CONTAINERS	US SENATOR JAKE GARN IS FIRST CIVILIAN POLITICIAN IN SPACE, SHOWING THAT YOU DO NOT HAVE TO BE SUPER-FIT TO FLY IN SPACE	YURI ROMANENKO COMPLETES 326 DAYS IN SPACE 1CM TALLER BUT WITH LEG MUSCLES 15 PER CENT SMALLER	VALERIY POLIYAKOV COMPLETES A RECORD-BREAKING 437-DAY STAY ON *MIR* SPACE STATION

Space station, 1971

The world's first space station – a base in **orbit** above the Earth permanently manned by people – was the **Soviet Union's** *Salyut 1*. Its inventors were the engineers who had designed the successful *Soyuz* spacecraft and the *Cosmos* satellites.

Long space-flights were needed to carry out scientific studies. To do this, **astronauts** had to spend several weeks in orbit, living inside a space laboratory or space station. In the future, space stations will also act as assembly points, to build large spacecraft setting out on long voyages to the planets. Doctors monitor space station astronauts to learn how the human body adapts to long periods in space, and also study the effects on other living things.

Longer and longer space-flights

The first manned spacecraft in 1961 spent only a few hours in orbit, but in June 1970 the Soviet *Soyuz 9* completed a flight of almost eighteen days. The first space station, *Salyut 1*, was launched in April 1971. Three **cosmonauts** were killed during their return trip to Earth after the first 23-day stay on *Salyut 1*. Despite this setback, however, by 1983 a further six *Salyuts* had been launched.

This 1995 photo shows a visiting Shuttle (bottom) docked with the Mir space station.

Salyut 6 in 1977 had two **docking** ports, so it could be resupplied and refuelled by either manned or **robot** spacecraft. *Salyut 7* in 1982 was even more successful. Long-stay cosmonauts spent over 300 days inside it. They received visits from *Soyuz* craft carrying fresh cosmonauts, and from unmanned *Progress* craft ferrying supplies.

The Americans decided to make use of leftover *Apollo* equipment to build their own space station, called *Skylab*. This 85-tonne orbital laboratory was launched by a *Saturn 5* rocket in 1973. It was visited by three teams of astronauts, the last team spending 84 days in space. It carried a spider, nicknamed

Arabella, which spun shapeless webs in zero **gravity** and some minnow fish, which swam in a spiral motion. *Apollo* Moon astronauts had suffered from colds and space sickness, but the *Skylab* flights showed that with exercise and better food, astronauts could stay fit and work for long periods.

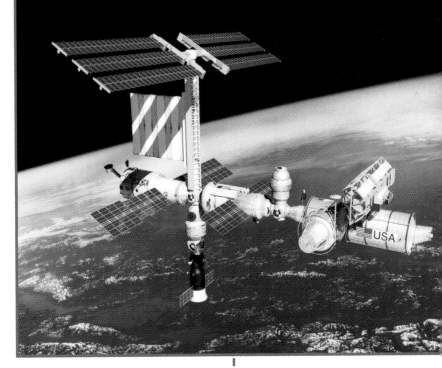

The International Space Station Alpha *is made up of sections assembled in orbit. It will be a permanent platform in space for science. The wing-like solar panels turn sunlight into electrical energy.*

Mir and the ISS

In 1986 the Soviets launched *Mir*, a much bigger station with six docking ports and room for six astronauts. It stayed in space until 2001. Even bigger will be the *International Space Station*, now being assembled in orbit. Work started in 1998 with the launch of two **modules**, one American and one Russian. Other parts are being built in Europe, Japan and Canada. The station will be visible in the night sky. You can access **NASA**'s Skywatch Internet site to find out when and where to look for it.

The International Space Station

The first crew of the *International Space Station* (ISS) were an American, Bill Shepherd, and two Russians, Yuri Gidzenko and Sergei Kinalev. In 2000 they celebrated the first Christmas in space by an *ISS* crew with a meal of **rehydrated** turkey. Four crews are in training. Each will spend 90 days aboard the space station. By 2003 the *ISS* should be complete, as new sections are brought up from Earth.

1971	1973	1983	1986	2001
SALYUT I IS WORLD'S FIRST SPACE STATION	THE USA LAUNCH *SKYLAB*	THE USA LAUNCH *SPACELAB*	SOVIET UNION LAUNCHES THE *MIR* SPACE STATION	ASTRONAUTS AT WORK ON THE *INTERNATIONAL SPACE STATION ALPHA*. *MIR* BURNS-UP AS IT RE-ENTERS EARTH'S ATMOSPHERE.

Mars lander, 1976

Mars is the only planet whose surface can be seen from Earth – clouds shroud Venus, our other near neighbour in the **solar system**. As it **orbits** the Sun, Mars comes to within 56 million kilometres of Earth, and to get there by spacecraft takes about six months.

Mars has fascinated scientists and science-fiction writers since 1877, when an Italian **astronomer** named Schiaparelli was reported as seeing 'canals' on the planet. He actually meant channels – lines on the dry surface – but the English word 'canals' suggested civilization, and many people were eager to believe in Martians! In 1898, H G Wells wrote of an invasion from Mars in his best-selling book *War of the Worlds.*

Going to Mars

In the early 1960s **NASA** started planning a manned Mars landing. In 1969 US Vice-President Agnew spoke of a landing 'by the end of the century', and NASA added a date for the epic expedition – 1982. It has not happened yet.

For now, **robots** are the best way to explore Mars. The Americans sent their first unmanned probes to Mars in 1965. In 1971 *Mariner 9* orbited the planet at a height of 1600 kilometres. From these missions, scientists learned much more about the planet's atmosphere, its two small moons and polar ice caps.

In 1976 the Viking landers sent back the first pictures of Mars taken from the surface. The photos showed a reddish, rock-strewn desert.

Landing on Mars

Mars has a thin atmosphere. It also has a rocky, dusty surface and landing can be tricky. A spacecraft must drop down slowly from orbit, using braking rockets, and finally relying on parachutes or inflated airbags to soften the landing. The first **soft-landing** on Mars was made by the Soviets in 1971. Their *Mars 3* orbiter released a capsule, but it stopped radioing signals after only 20 seconds.

Scientists got their first close-up look at Mars in 1976, when the American space probes *Viking 1* and 2 landed safely using parachutes. They sent back photographs of a wind-scoured desert with sand dunes and sharp rocks. In one photo some people thought they could see a huge rock-carved 'face'. Clearer photos in 1998 by the *Mars Global Surveyor* probe showed that the face was a natural feature, shaped by the wind. In 1997 the *Pathfinder* lander placed the first robot explorer on Mars, the six-wheeled *Sojourner* crawler.

Two US Viking *spacecraft like this one landed on Mars in 1976, after a ten-month journey from Earth.* Vikings 1 *and* 2 *landed about 6,500 kilometres apart.*

Life on Mars?

Scientists know that Mars is cold and has no **oxygen**. So far scientific tests on its soil have failed to reveal any signs of life, now or in the past. A claim in 1996 that fossil bacteria had been found in Mars rocks was not accepted by all scientists. Scientists want to send spacecraft to look for water on Mars. If water still exists, there might once have been life on Mars. Perhaps future **astronauts** will be able to use Martian water and even mine chemicals to make rocket fuel for the return trip.

1969	1971	1976	1988	1998
US *MARINER 6* PROBE REVEALS THAT MARS HAS CRATERS, LIKE THE MOON	*MARINER 9* ORBITS MARS AND FINDS IT COVERED BY A HUGE DUST STORM	*VIKING 1* AND 2 LAND ON MARS	TWO SOVIET PROBES TO MARS' MOON PHOBOS FAIL	*MARS CLIMATE ORBITER* BURNS UP ON ENTERING THE MARTIAN ATMOSPHERE – BECAUSE ENGINEERS ON EARTH MUDDLED UP IMPERIAL AND METRIC UNITS WHEN DOING THEIR SUMS!

Space Shuttle, 1981

The Space Shuttle is the cargo truck of space. It flies up into **orbit**, carrying satellites, people, space station equipment, and scientific experiments. Unlike a rocket, this winged spacecraft can be used again and again.

Into space and back again

Inventors have designed 'rocket-planes' to fly into space and back again. In comic books and space movies, rockets usually shoot straight up into space and land back on Earth – often tail first, belching smoke and flames. A real space rocket cannot do this. A rocket re-entering the atmosphere glows red-hot as it meets the **friction** from the air. As it drops lower, it needs parachutes to slow its descent, unless it has wings and can glide down like an aeroplane.

The space liner

In the 1970s US engineers built the first winged spacecraft, the Space Shuttle. It first flew in 1981. About the size of a medium-sized airliner, the shuttle takes off vertically, attached to a giant fuel tank filled with liquid hydrogen and liquid **oxygen** to feed its engines. Two solid-fuel rocket boosters provide extra power for take-off. They drop off when empty and fall back to Earth to be used again. The spacecraft roars on, burning the fuel in its big tank. This then also falls away while the Shuttle flies into orbit about 300 kilometres above Earth.

To survive the fierce heat of re-entry, the Shuttle is shielded by ceramic tiles, which absorb the heat. As it meets the air, it begins to gain lift from its wings, and glides

The Space Shuttle has a huge cargo bay, and an extending mechanical arm for releasing and capturing satellites.

down to land on a runway. Despite one disaster, in 1986, the Shuttle has proved very reliable. The United States has a fleet of four craft.

In future, smaller shuttle craft, such as the proposed *X-38* crew return vehicle, could serve as 'rescue ships' to pick up **astronauts** from the *International Space Station*, should an emergency arise. In the 1980s the **Soviet Union** also designed a shuttle, known as *Buran*, which was to be launched by the huge *Energia* rocket. However, this programme was abandoned.

Sally Ride, seen here inside the Shuttle Challenger *in 1983, was the first American woman astronaut. During the six-day flight, she helped launch two satellites and tested the remote manipulator arm (shown on page 38). She made a second Shuttle flight in 1984.*

Sally Ride (b. 1951)

Sally Ride of the USA was the third woman in space, and the first American woman. Born in California in 1951, she studied physics at Stanford University. In 1979 she was assigned to the Shuttle programme and in 1983 she made her first flight aboard *Challenger*. It was the first five-person mission. She was back in orbit the following year, also on *Challenger*, and this time one of a record seven-person crew. She later served on the commission of inquiry into the 1986 explosion which destroyed *Challenger* and killed seven American astronauts. In 1987 she left **NASA** to continue her academic life as a scientist.

1981	1986	1988	1988	1990	1998
FIRST SHUTTLE MISSION BY COLUMBIA	USA'S WORST SPACE TRAGEDY, WHEN SHUTTLE *CHALLENGER* EXPLODES, KILLING ALL SEVEN CREW	SHUTTLE FLIGHTS RESUME AFTER CHANGES IN DESIGN	TRIALS BEGIN OF THE SOVIET *BURAN* SHUTTLE, LATER ABANDONED	SHUTTLE LAUNCHES HUBBLE SPACE TELESCOPE	SHUTTLE LAUNCHES FIRST US SECTION OF *INTERNATIONAL SPACE STATION*

Jet pack, 1984

To get around in space, weightless and airless, an **astronaut** must become a miniature spacecraft, with a personal propulsion and guidance system – a jet pack.

The first astronauts did not move from their cramped capsules. By the mid-1960s scientists were eager to see how well people could work in space, leaving the craft and venturing outside, protected only by their spacesuits.

The first space-walks

The first person to try a space-walk was Soviet **cosmonaut** Aleksei Leonov. In March 1965 he emerged from the airlock of *Voskhod 2* and spent ten minutes outside, tied to the spacecraft by a safety line. US *Gemini 4* astronaut Ed White repeated the feat in June 1965. He experimented with a small handheld 'gas-gun' (a bit like a water pistol, firing gas) to push himself around. This was the first American extra-vehicular activity (EVA) – **NASA** jargon for walking in space.

To do work in space, such as setting up experiments and doing repairs, astronauts need freedom to move about easily. In zero **gravity**, every move has to be made with care. Push against the side of the craft and a floating astronaut will begin to drift away. In the same way, a jet of gas squirted in one direction produces a force in the opposite direction. A propulsion system for floating in space needed to be simple and ultra-reliable, for one mistake could send an untethered astronaut flying off into empty space, with no hope of rescue.

*American astronaut Ed White during his 21-minute space-walk in 1965. He is holding his **oxygen**-powered 'gas-gun'.*

A narrow escape

EVAs can be dangerous, so astronauts maintain a close watch on any colleague working outside. Soviet cosmonaut Yuri Romanenko had a narrow escape in 1977, during his first space-flight aboard *Soyuz 26*. He left the cabin for a space walk, but failed to check that his safety line was secured. The absent-minded Romanenko would have floated off into space had his quick-thinking partner Georgi Grechko not grabbed the line and hauled him in, like an oversized space fish!

The MMU

In the 1980s NASA engineers developed a 'flying chair', known as the Manned Manoeuvring Unit or MMU for short, for use on Shuttle missions. It was first tried by astronaut Bruce McCandless in February 1984. He wore it for 90 minutes, flying completely free of the Shuttle more than 350 kilometres above the Pacific Ocean. He was able to move gently in any direction, firing short bursts of nitrogen gas from the unit's eight sets of thrusters. An astronaut steers the MMU with hand controllers in the 'arms'. Nitrogen gas is stored in tanks in the backpack. The MMU has no safety line, so the astronaut's life depends entirely on the reliability of its systems.

Astronauts of the 21st century fly free, using the MMU – the fastest 'armchair' in or out of this world. While using the MMU, the astronaut becomes a living satellite, travelling around the world at the same speed as the spacecraft to which he or she returns when the space-walk is over. Astronauts use their jet packs to move around outside the spacecraft, working on satellites or sections of space station.

1965	1965	1984	1984	1990s	2001
FIRST SPACE-WALK, BY ALEKSEI LEONOV OF THE **SOVIET UNION**	US ASTRONAUT ED WHITE TRIES OUT A HANDHELD 'SPACE GUN' TO HELP HIM MOVE ABOUT IN WEIGHTLESSNESS	SVETLANA SAVITSKAYA OF THE SOVIET UNION IS FIRST WOMAN TO WALK IN SPACE	SHUTTLE ASTRONAUT BRUCE MCCANDLESS TRIES OUT MANNED MANOEUVRING UNIT (MMU)	SHUTTLE ASTRONAUTS MOVE ABOUT IN SHUTTLE CARGO BAY TO LAUNCH SATELLITES AND RECOVER FAULTY ONES FOR REPAIR	SPACE STATION CREWS USE MMUS WHILE ASSEMBLING THE NEW *INTERNATIONAL SPACE STATION*

Space telescope, 1990

The telescope is quite an old invention – Galileo used one in 1609. Telescopes have become less useful on Earth, however, because of the pollution created by city lights, car exhausts, factory smoke and television signals. To get a really clear view of the stars and planets, scientists send telescopes and other instruments into space itself.

Astronauts *working on the Hubble space telescope during the 1993 shuttle mission which successfully repaired Hubble's faulty 'eye'.*

Looking for heat in space

The first infra-red telescope for use in astronomy was invented by American scientist Frank J Low in 1961. It warmed up slightly every time it detected infra-red rays from outer space. When an infra-red telescope was sent into space on board the *Infra-Red Astronomy Satellite* (*IRAS*) in 1983, it began searching for distant stars so cold that they give off no visible light. It found over 200,000 infra-red sources in the ten months it kept working. An infra-red telescope like *IRAS* has to be chilled down almost to absolute zero (-273°C) so that no 'haze' of heat from the telescope itself interferes with the heat-rays it is picking up from distant stars.

The Hubble telescope

The biggest space telescope yet is the Hubble telescope. Named after America's greatest **astronomer**, it is as big as a truck. It was placed in **orbit** about 600 kilometres above the Earth by the Shuttle *Discovery* in 1990. It circles the Earth roughly every 90 minutes.

Hubble was designed to send back pictures of stars ten times clearer than the biggest telescopes on Earth can give. Astronomers were disappointed when the first pictures proved fuzzy. The telescope's mirror was flawed. At the factory, it had been ground to the wrong shape – a very expensive mistake! At first, engineers did their best to enhance, or sharpen, the pictures, using computers to correct the fuzzy images. Then, it was decided to 'recapture' and repair Hubble. This was done in 1993 by sending the Space Shuttle *Endeavour* to intercept the giant telescope in orbit. The *Endeavour*'s crew succeeded in installing a new device with ten tiny mirrors and a new camera to correct the fault in the mirror. Hubble began sending back brilliant pictures, more detailed than any that can be seen from Earth.

Thanks to the engineers' ingenuity, Hubble gives Earth-bound astronomers their clearest view yet of the universe. It can peer into the heart of **galaxies**, looking for evidence of **black holes**. It has taken pictures of stars more than 100 million **light years** away from us. Even bigger space telescopes with mirrors designed to unfold up to 8 metres across will be launched in the next few years.

Edwin Hubble (1889–1953)

As a young student, Edwin Hubble was inspired to study the stars by astronomer George E Hale, who has a large land-based telescope in California named after him. Working at the Mount Wilson Laboratory in California, Hubble discovered that distant galaxies are moving away from us at an increasing speed. Before this discovery, scientists had thought the universe was static – unchanging. Hubble's observations and calculations showed that it was expanding, most probably as a consequence of the Big Bang – the explosion of energy in which the universe began.

1958	1962	1973	1983	1990	1999
EXPLORER I MAKES FIRST ASTRONOMICAL OBSERVATIONS FROM SPACE	ORBITING SOLAR OBSERVATORY LAUNCHED TO STUDY RADIATION FROM THE SUN	APOLLO TELESCOPE MOUNT CARRIED ON US SKYLAB SPACE STATION	IRAS INFRA-RED ASTRONOMY SATELLITE FINDS NEW STARS	HUBBLE SPACE TELESCOPE IS FIRST LARGE TELESCOPE IN SPACE	EUROPEAN XMM (X-RAY MULTI MIRROR) TELESCOPE LAUNCHED BY ARIANE ROCKET

Timeline

AD 1000	By this date Chinese have learned how to make **gunpowder**
1241	Tartar army fires rockets at Polish troops – perhaps Europe's first taste of rocket warfare
1609	Galileo discovers Jupiter's four largest moons with the aid of his telescope
1668	Sir Isaac Newton builds first reflector telescope with a mirror to collect light
1850s	First photographs of the Moon taken from Earth by William C Bond and J A Whipple of Harvard University
1926	Robert Goddard test-fires world's first liquid-fuelled rocket
1935	A 'Goddard' rocket flies faster than sound
1937	Grote Reber builds first working radio telescope
1957	**Soviet Union** launches the first satellites – *Sputnik 1* and *Sputnik 2*
1958	*Explorer 1*, first US satellite, launched by a *Jupiter C* rocket
1959	Soviet space probe, *Luna 2*, is first to hit the Moon
1960s	Radio **astronomers** discover quasars – the most distant objects detected from Earth
1960	*Tiros 1* is first weather satellite
1960	US Navy launches first *Transit* Navigation Satellite
1961	Yuri Gagarin flies into history on board *Vostok 1*, the world's first manned spacecraft
1963	Soviet **cosmonaut** Valentina Tereshkova is first woman in space
1965	Aleksei Leonov is first person to make a space-walk wearing a spacesuit

1969
A *Saturn 5* rocket sends *Apollo 11* spacecraft on its historic trip to the Moon

Apollo 11 **astronauts** Neil Armstrong and Edwin 'Buzz' Aldrin land on the Moon

1970
The Soviet Union's *Lunokhod* is first **robot** explorer on the Moon, and its *Venera 7* is first probe to survive landing on Venus

1971
The Soviet Union's *Salyut 1* is world's first space station

1972
Landsat is first Earth-resources satellite

1976
Viking 1 lands on Mars on July 20, *Viking 2* follows on September 3

1978
United States launches first *Navstar* satellites, setting up a global navigation system

1981
First Space Shuttle mission, by Columbia

1984
Shuttle astronaut Bruce McCandless tries out Manned Manoeuvring Unit

1986
USA's worst space tragedy, when Shuttle *Challenger* explodes 73 seconds after take-off, killing all seven crew

Soviets launch their *Mir* Space Station

1990
Hubble Space Telescope is first large telescope in space

1995
Valeriy Poliyakov completes 437 days on *Mir*, the longest stay in space to date

1997
USA's *Sojourner* robot crawls on Mars, studying rocks

2001
Astronauts at work on board the *International Space Station*, which is being assembled in stages

Glossary

antenna device for collecting electrical and radio signals in the atmosphere, also called an aerial

astronaut person trained to fly in space. The name comes from Greek words meaning 'star-sailor'.

astronomer scientist who studies the stars and other objects in space

barometer instrument for measuring air pressure

black hole all that remains of a collapsed star. It is a tiny object with such great mass that not even light can escape the pull of its gravity, so it is invisible.

Cold War period of hostility between the West (the USA and its allies) and the Communist world (Soviet Union and China and their allies), which lasted from the 1940s to the 1980s

concave curved shape like the inside of a bowl

convex curved shape like the outside of a bowl

cosmonaut name used by Soviet space scientists for their first astronauts. Comes from Greek words meaning 'sailor of the universe'.

crater pit or hole made in the surface of the Moon or another body such as a planet by a meteorite crashing into it

disarmament giving up weapons (arms)

docking joining together spacecraft in space, using gentle rocket thrusts to steer one craft into a locking attachment on the other craft

electronics using the flow of electrical charges to make useful devices such as computers and televisions.

escape velocity speed a spacecraft must reach to escape the gravity of a planet and travel away into deep space

friction force that tries to stop one surface sliding or rolling against another. Friction makes spacecraft become hot when they re-enter the Earth's atmosphere.

galaxy group or system of stars. There are billions of galaxies in the universe, and ours is called the Milky Way.

geostationary orbit 'fixed position' orbit for a satellite. At about 35,900 km high a satellite moves around the Earth at the same speed as the Earth is spinning, so from the ground the satellite appears to stay still.

gravity force that pulls all objects towards the surface of the Earth or any other planet, moon or star

gunpowder the first explosive

gyroscope spinning device for keeping balance. Gyroscopes are fitted in navigation systems for aircraft, missiles and spacecraft.

integrated circuit electronic device made up of thousands of miniature parts wired together on a slice of silicon material, known as a chip

laser device that produces a narrow but very strong beam of light. Can be used to send television signals.

lens curved piece of glass or other transparent material which lets light through it, either converging (bringing together) or diverging (spreading) the rays

light year unit used to describe distances between stars. Light travels at 299,792 kilometres every second, so in a year light travels a very long way – about 9.5 million million kilometres.

missile anything thrown or fired, such as a stone, arrow or bullet

module part of a larger piece of equipment or system

National Aeronautics and Space Administration (NASA) US government organization set up in 1958 to run the United States' space programme

nuclear weapon bomb with enormous destructive power, obtained by changing matter into energy

orbit path followed by a satellite around the Earth, and by planets around a star such as the Sun

oxygen gas found in air, essential to human life

payload the useful load a rocket can lift into orbit or send on a spaceflight – such as a satellite, probe with scientific instruments, or craft carrying people

radar system for tracking objects or measuring how fast they are travelling. It uses radio beams which bounce off an object and travel back to a receiver.

radiation giving off energy in the form of light, electricity or heat. The stars give out various forms of energy which travel through space as rays.

radio ham someone who uses a home radio to talk with or send code messages to other radio amateurs.

reflection the bouncing back of light rays or sound waves as they hit a surface

refraction the bending of light rays as they pass from one substance to another, for instance, from air to water

rehydrated when water has been added to a substance (such as dried food) to bring it back to its original form

robot machine that carries out tasks it has been taught, or that can be controlled by a computer or a person

rotation turning or spinning motion, moving in a circle like a wheel

soft-landing controlled descent onto a moon or planet, using rockets, parachutes or airbags

solar system the Sun and the nine planets, including Earth, which orbit it

Soviet Union federation of communist republics led by Russia until break-up in 1991

spectroscope special telescope for studying the spectrum of light from stars

step rocket rocket in two or three sections. Each section has its own engines, and falls off when its fuel is used up.

sunspot cooler, dark patch on the surface of the Sun.

Index

Apollo spacecraft 23, 24, 27, 29, 35
astronomers 8, 10, 13

Big Bang 43
black holes 43

Challenger 39
Cold War 20
Copernicus, Nicolaus 8

docking missions 23

electronics 5, 16, 21, 28
escape velocity 16
extra-vehicular activity (EVA) 40-1

food and drink 32-3, 35
friction 17, 38

Gagarin, Yuri 22, 23, 24 25, 32
galaxies 5, 13, 43
Galileo 8, 9, 42
geostationary orbit 18, 19
Gilruth, Robert 23
Glenn, John 23
Global Positioning System 21
Goddard, Robert H 10, 11
gravity 4, 10, 14, 16, 31, 33, 40
gyroscopes 17

health in space 33, 35

Herschel, William 9
Hubble, Edwin 43
Hubble Space Telescope 9, 21, 42-3

International Space Station 5, 35, 39

Jansky, Karl 12
jet packs 40, 41
Jodrell Bank 13
Jupiter 8, 17

Manned Manoeuvring Unit (MMU) 41
manned spacecraft 22-3, 29, 30, 31, 34-5, 38-9
Mars 31, 36-7
Mir space station 33, 34, 35
missiles 10, 15, 20, 23, 26
Moon 8, 17, 26, 27, 28, 29, 30, 31

NASA 15, 17, 21, 23, 25, 27, 28, 31, 35, 36, 39, 41
Newton, Sir Isaac 7, 9, 14

Oberth, Hermann 10, 11, 14
orbit 4, 8, 14, 16, 18, 20, 34, 36, 38, 42
oxygen 10, 25, 26, 30, 37, 38

radar 5, 17, 20
radiation 12, 17, 25
Reber, Grote 13
Ride, Sally 39
robot explorers 30, 31, 36, 37
rockets 5, 6-7, 10-11, 14,16, 20, 26, 27, 38

satellites 5, 14, 15, 18-19, 20-1, 42
Saturn 5 rocket 26, 27, 28
Skylab 27, 34-5
solar system 5, 17, 36
space probes 16-17, 31, 36, 37
space race 5, 16, 20, 28
space shuttles 23, 25, 38-9, 42, 43
space sickness 33, 35
space stations 25, 34-5
space-walks 24, 25, 40-1
spectroscopes 17
Sputnik 14, 15, 22
sunspots 8

telescopes 4, 5, 8-9, 12-13, 42-3
Tsiolkovski, Konstantin 10, 11

Van Allen, James 15
Von Braun, Wernher 26, 27